Yogi Ferrell in?

Author: Dana Hoopingarner

Co-Author: Kevin "Yogi" Ferrell

Illustrator: Kevin Gillum

Volume #1

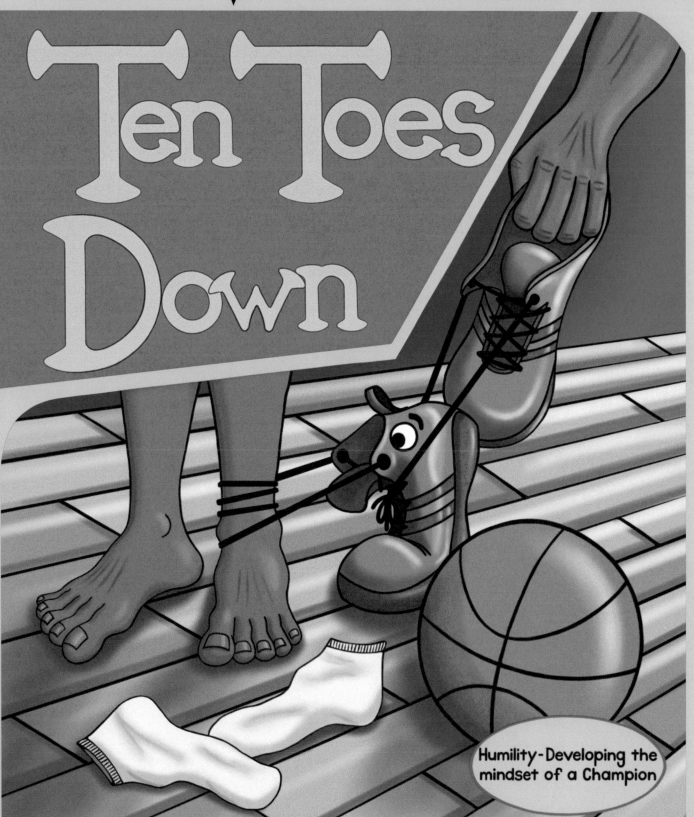

Ten Toes Down

Humility-Developing the mindset of a Champion

AuthorHouse™
1663 Liberty Drive
Bloomington, IN 47403
www.authorhouse.com
Phone: 1 (800) 839-8640

Artwork by Kevin Gillum, Kevin Gillum Illustrations kevingillum.illustrations@gmail.com

Published by AuthorHouse 6/4/2019

ISBN: 978-1-5462-7932-7 (sc)
ISBN: 978-1-5462-7934-1 (hc)
ISBN: 978-1-5462-7933-4 (e)

Library of Congress Control Number: 2019901333

Print information available on the last page.

authorHOUSE®

BASKETBALL SLANG GLOSSARY

Hardwood–Basketball Court

Downtown–Refers to the area behind the three-point line. Any basket that is scored beyond the three-point line, or downtown, is worth three points.

Rack Up The Numbers–Scoring many points for the team

Burying The Jumper–Shooting and making the basket in a jump shot

Crashing The Boards–This is another way to describe rebounding in basketball. The term "boards" is the reference to the backboard and "crashing" refers to moving aggressively and quickly to rebound the basketball

Dunk–A basketball shot that is performed when a player jumps in the air, with one or both hands on the basketball, controlling the ball above the rim, and scores by directly putting the ball through the basket

Egotistical–Given to talking about oneself; vain; boastful; opinionated

Montrosity–An object of great and often frightening size, force, or complexity

Dance The Defense–Two people pretending to steal and deflect passes with fancy footwork

Rock–Basketball

Driving The Lane–The ball handler will penetrate the lane with the basketball, dribbling it in the middle of the free throw area to the basket. This is an offensive move. The hope is that the defensive team will be drawn away from the basket as the offensive team spreads out over half court to open "the lane".

Trey–Three-point basket

ogi opened the door to the local church gymnasium and took a deep breath. The smell of sweaty socks, the sound of squeaking shoes, and a blowing referee whistle made his heart skip a beat. There was nothing in the world more important than being on the "hardwood" with his friends in a pick-up game.

"Yogi!" yelled Downtown. "Where have you been? Did your Mama have you doin' that choir boy-singing again today?"

"No." Yogi said with a grin. "Just working on my handstand."

Downtown rocked with laughter as he watched Yogi dribble out to the free throw line and drop down into his handstand. Yogi usually had so much focus on the court but lately had been clowning around until the whistle blew to begin. It wasn't like Yogi to be so loose about workouts. He was the best player that Downtown had ever seen. He could hit a 3-pointer better than many players that were older than him...All...Day...Long! He could rack up the numbers. Yogi was ranked top Fourth Grade player in the *Players Press*, so if he wanted to joke around a bit, it must be ok!

Downtown could hit a shot from half court, which is how he got his nickname, but Yogi was the best all-around player. Lately, though.... Yogi was acting strange.

The whistle blew and the pick-up game started and ended. Yogi had 33 points that game.

Yogi and Downtown walked out of the gym with goals and expectations met for the day. They had won. No doubt about it, they were the team above every team.

"Did you see me?" boasted Yogi. "I couldn't miss!"

"Yeah. I saw you. EVERYBODY saw you," muttered Downtown.

"You couldn't miss you. EVERYBODY heard you. 'I'm open. I'm open.'"

Yogi froze in his tracks abruptly and folded his arms across his chest.

"What are you talkin' about? I am the best player out there. Just look my stats up online!"

"What's wrong with you, Yogi! Don't you remember what your Pops taught you. What he taught all of us?" questioned Downtown.

First get your teammates involved, then get yourself involved.

Yogi was annoyed with this whole conversation. "Of course, I remember what he said,

'First get your teammates involved, then get yourself involved.'

I have it written in my locker AND my bedroom."

"Well, you better read it again. Read it nice and slow this time. You are thinking a lot of yourself these days and there are four other players on the court with you. Ya know, I love ya man, but I think you are getting a big head." Downtown gave Yogi a slap on the back and jetted down the street.

Yogi was good and he knew it. He wasn't going to let Downtown's words get to him. He knew what he was doing. He knew he was the best. He knew nobody was better than him.

Yogi flew in the living room and plopped on the couch where his Pops and brother were eating a snack. "How did the game go, Son?" asked his father.

"Super! I am the best! I scored 33 points. Nobody could stop me, Pop!" announced Yogi.

"Hmmm.... really. How did your team do? Did you all work together well?" questioned his father. "I guess so. We won," said Yogi with a shrug.

Yogi's brother jumped up with a frustrated look on his face and pointed out to Yogi the obvious.

"You think you are so good, Yogi! I bet there are a lot of kids your age that are better than you. You haven't even met them yet! If you don't watch out, you are going to wake up one day to a humongous head full of all your own thoughts about you, you, YOU!"

"Hey! Just look up my stats on the internet! I'm famous!" announced Yogi.

Yogi's father gave him a serious look. "Well, Mr. Famous, the trash needs to be taken out. We can talk about this all later."

Yogi's father watched his son go out the door with the trash. "At what point did he become so arrogant and self-centered?" he asked himself. *Confidence and bravery are needed for success, yet crossing the line and becoming egotistical is a bad vibe. Hmmm...It may just be time for a lesson called, Ten Toes Down,* he thought to himself.

Yogi went to bed thinking of the day. It felt bitter sweet. It was not quite the reaction he expected from his best friend and family after scoring 33 points.

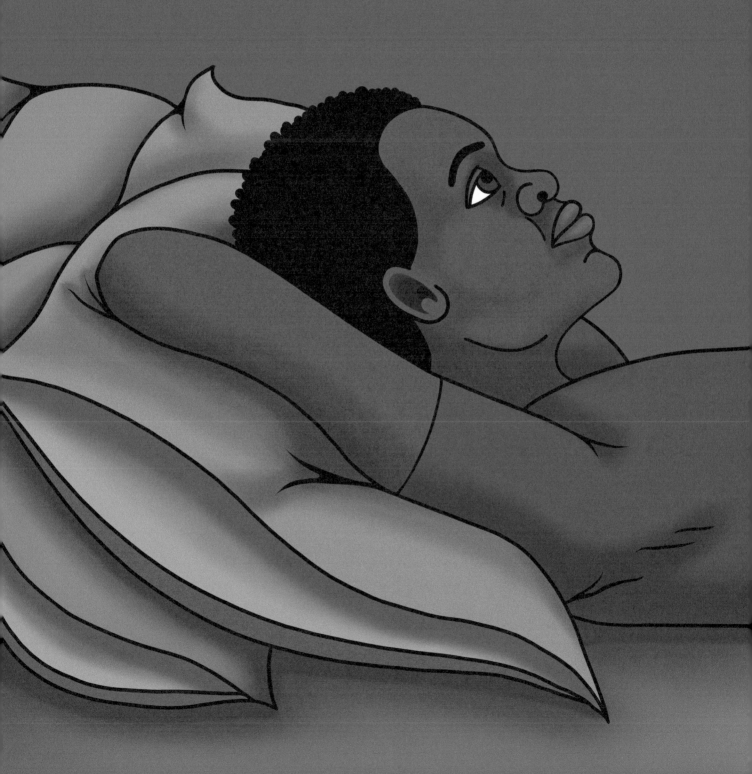

Yogi drifted off to sleep. His night's sleep took him into the next day with a headache. He didn't want it to spoil his gym time so he went to quickly dress and brush his teeth, hopeful it would go away. Glancing in the bathroom mirror, Yogi was shocked by what he saw.

"Ahhhhhhhhh......my head. My head is big!" he screamed. "I have A BIG HEAD!"

Yogi couldn't believe his eyes. It was true. All those thoughts about himself made his head grow. His body was the same size but his head..... ohhhhh.....his head, was...well....ummm...HUGE!

He ran into his bedroom and grabbed a hat. Maybe his hat would cover his big ol' head.

No! It didn't fit. He grabbed a lampshade. Placing it strategically and carefully on his head, he pretended not to notice it was there. It was a no go. It would not be ignored.

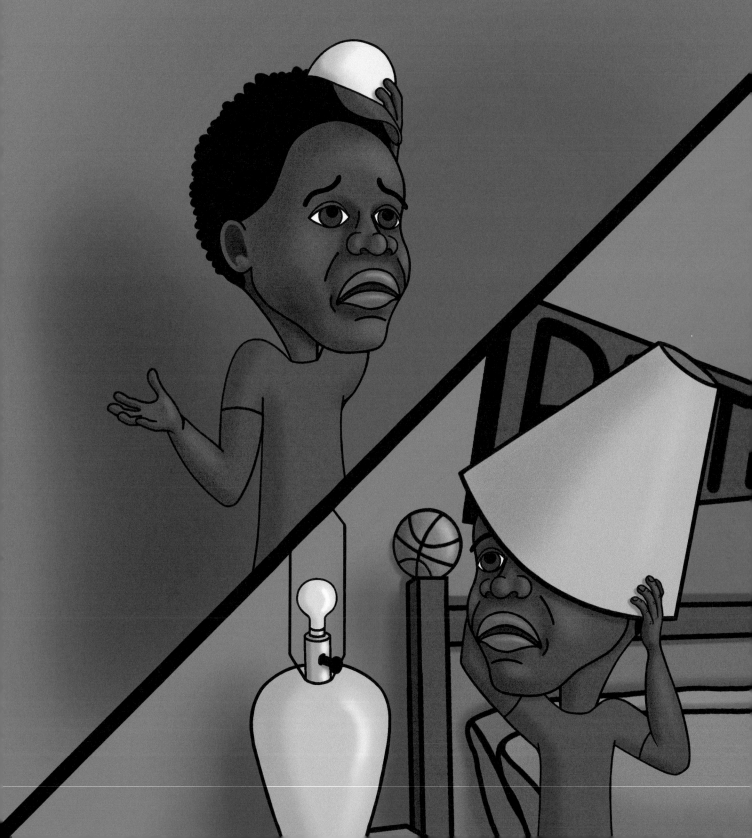

He grabbed his pet cat, Bubbles, gave her a snuggle, and placed her on top of his head. Like a well-balanced book, Bubbles laid on Yogi's head and stretched her little legs over his ears. Yogi pulled her little feet this way and that way, trying to hide the monstrosity of his cranium.

No! No! No! Nothing was working.

As a last resort Yogi grabbed his red and white hoodie and began to slip it over his head. Carefully pulling it down, the neck hole seemed to be small. How could this be? This was his favorite college hoodie. He had worn this hoodie a thousand times. It had never been too small for him. It grew tighter and tighter around his head. Franticly, he began to wrestle with his sweatshirt pulling and tugging, stretching and yanking with all his might. Up and down, to the left and to the right, Yogi yanked. This...was... NOT...working! He was stuck in the neck of his favorite college sweatshirt. Stuck! Stuck! Stuck! His big head was stuck!

"Yogi," yelled his mama, "time for breakfast!"

Yogi could feel his heart melting inside with embarrassment as he remembered all the words he had spoken about himself. Those arrogant words flooded his mind. "I am great!" "I'm famous!" Oh! How he wished he would've never said those words out loud!

The realization of what his brother and Downtown had claimed was clear. It was as they said. He now had a big head.

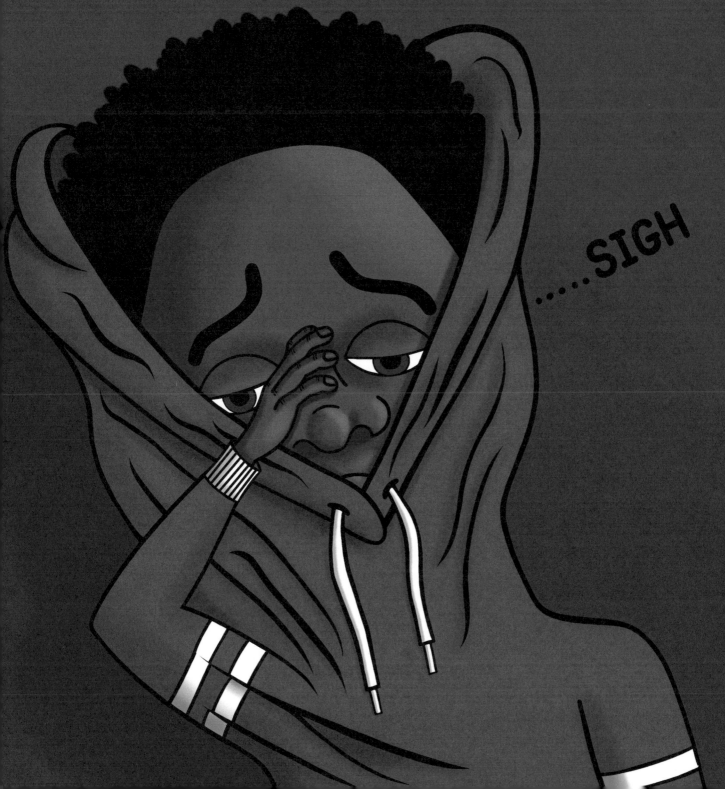

Yogi could hear his mama coming up the stairs to his bedroom. She would soon see his dilemma - his big head. How was he going to explain this mess he had gotten himself into?

Yogi found that being stuck in his hoodie helped him think better. He felt his heart settle down and held his breath awaiting his mama's screams at the sight of his big head.

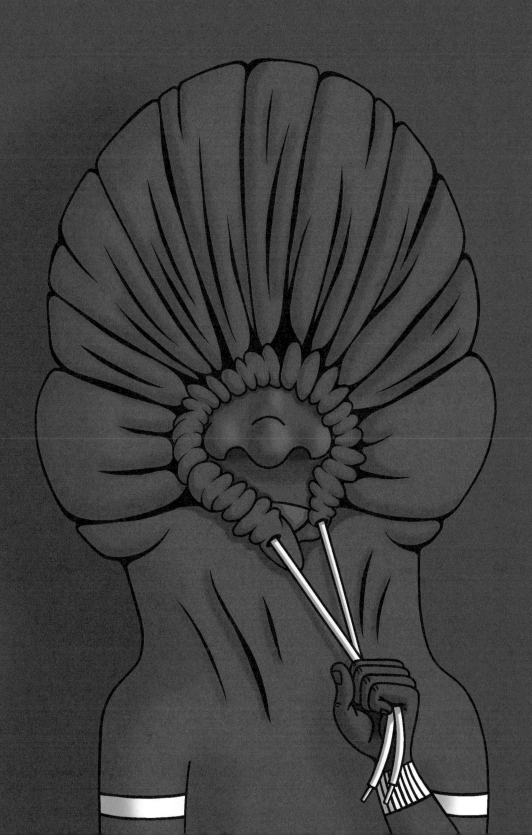

"Yogi! Son! Get yourself up outta that bed and get yourself dressed!"

Yogi opened his eyes. He grabbed his head. Yogi sat straight up and began touching every part of his face, ears and hairline. His head was normal! It had all been a dream! Jumping out of bed he threw his arms around her waist. His head wasn't big at all. It had all been a very bad dream.

"Mama? What exactly is it when someone gets a 'big head'? I mean, how do you know that you're starting to get one of those?"

Yogi's mother began to explain, "Well, Yogi, a big head is considered arrogance. It is when you start to boast and brag with your own mouth. People will even puff out their chest like a peacock, which is a sign of being overly confident. Someone that goes on and on about how great they are and making everyone else feel like they are nothing is a sign of big headedness."

"Another example is when your thoughts continue to repeat that you are better and bigger than anyone around you. That is the beginning of becoming full of pride. It is disappointing when words like that are heard out of someone's mouth."

Yogi looked up at his mama and nodded. His stomach let out a growl that drew attention to how hungry he was.

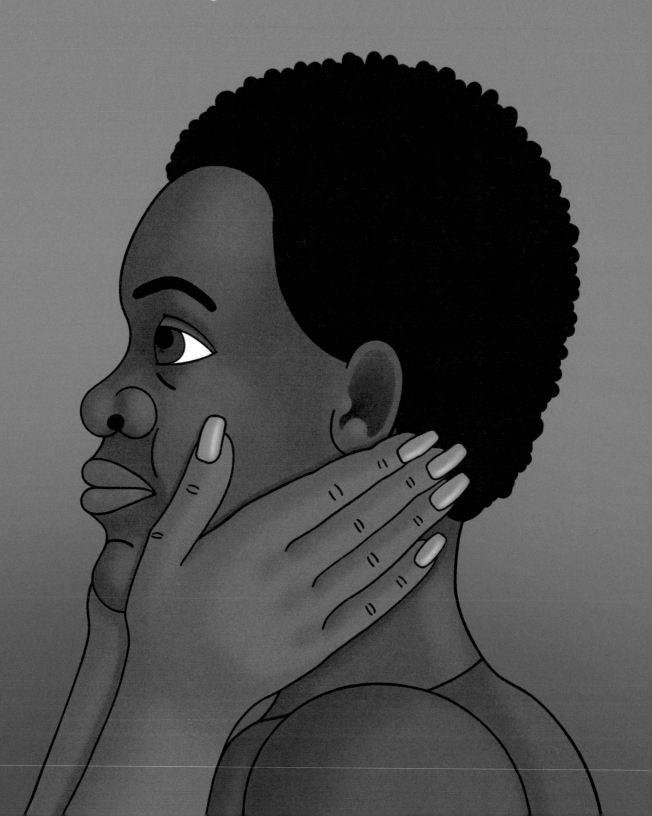

Yogi followed the smell of the pancakes, slid down the banister and landed in the breakfast chair with a thump. He grabbed a mountain of pancakes.

"Hey! Pop!" piped Yogi. Pop looked over the top of his coffee cup and watched his son carefully roll each pancake into a tube.

"Good Morning, Son! What are you doing to your pancakes?"

Taking the pancake and pretending to shoot it like a basketball into the maple syrup, Yogi flashed a toothy grin at his Pop and snickered, "I'm learning how to "dunk"!"

They both burst out into laughter that rang through the house. Yogi loved to joke around. He finished his breakfast and grabbed his basketball ready to get his minutes on the court. Pop laid his hand on top of Yogi's head as he passed by.

"I want you to remember this today, Son! You may be very good at burying a jumper but another person might crash the boards in rebounds. Together you make a great team. All working toward the common goal of winning a ballgame. It is better to just do your job and stay humble. A humble heart is responsive, ready to listen and learn. Like yours is right now. 'Out of the heart, the mouth speaks.' What you are thinking about throughout the day, what is in your heart, will eventually come out of your mouth. Thinking of others first and thinking good things about teammates will always make you a winner!"

Yogi and his Pops began to "dance the defense" – a tradition that was used when one of them left the house for the day.

It was an unspoken way to communicate how much they loved each other without saying it. Pops began to make his move around Yogi in a pretend lay-up. Yogi dramatically fell to the ground, arms flying and legs up in the air, yelling "FOUL!" Cracking up in laughter Pops helped Yogi up. His father squared up Yogi's shoulders and looked him in the eye.

"Ten Toes Down, Yogi," said his father firmly.

Yogi knew just what that meant. It was one of their favorite sayings. Ten Toes Down are a sign of commitment and total devotion. It meant to not only stay grounded and on guard, but to stand firm with your feet planted. Yogi applied it here and giving his father 100% of his attention. He declared, "I'm Ten Toes Down, Pop!"

His father continued, "Being brave and confident are good qualities for any ball player to have. It makes you a force to be reckoned with on the court. You will move and jump the way others won't because of that courage and confidence. It goes wrong when it becomes all about you and your eyes don't see anybody else but you. That will create a big foul! The whistle will blow and the game will stop for a minute. Sometimes, that is just what we need, to get back in focus and get our emotions in control. So, I am blowing the whistle, Yogi. It's time for you to stop the game for a while and get your focus on. Do you understand?"

"I think so. Do you mean I can never play basketball? You are making me quit the game?" Yogi couldn't hide the quiver in his voice. He got it. He was right in the middle of one of those life lessons. This felt TERRIBLE!

Yogi's father gently patted his son on the back, with a smile. "You'll be alright sitting it out for a while. You were made to shine. Basketball found you. You were made to do this. For now though, let's refocus and look around a bit. Let's experience having some fun with family! We have all missed you since you have been at the gym so much. There is plenty of time for shooting the rock."

Yogi was stunned. He couldn't move. What would he do now? Not playing basketball had never been a thought for him. He needed to talk to Downtown.

Yogi found Downtown on the park bench and shared all the happenings of the last 24 hours with him, including his dream about having a big head. Yogi apologized for his attitude and Downtown acted like it was no big deal. Yogi admired how Downtown could make an awkward situation feel... well...not awkward. Saying you're sorry can be a bit embarrassing but totally cool all at the same time!

Downtown listened to all that Yogi had to say. He shook his head and said, "Yogi, my man, hang tough. You will be back driving the lane in no time! There will always be a spot for you on our team. Until then, Ten Toes Down!

The two buddies looped arms and began to walk to the corner deli for their favorite juice. There was nothing like best friends. In Yogi's opinion, Downtown, who would soon grow to be seven feet tall, just hit another "trey".

THE END!

ABOUT THE AUTHOR

Dana Hoopingarner or "Mrs. Dana" as her students call her, has been in the education field for 30 years. Her desire to teach through children's books and engage young minds into creative thinkers is a continual goal. Conversations held in her classroom over the years, has given her a unique writers eye and an ear to hear the laughter in the words of the little storytellers. Bringing good-natured lessons that apply for today's youth, and an awareness to help children learn to stand without fear in difficult circumstances and situations, is the platform from within her writings. Mrs. Dana loves that her readers find a new awakening of courage when reading her work. Filling libraries with stacks of books that help inspire good choices is an honor she holds of high regard. Mrs. Dana has been married to her high-school sweetheart for 36 years, has three married children and eight grandchildren. She has written three books in The Stinky Feet Book Series and resides in Indiana.

ABOUT THE ILLUSTRATOR

Kevin Gillum has recently ventured into the world of professional illustrating, excitingly this is his first children's book project. Creating the right look for a young "Yogi" Ferrell and all the color and imagery that this children's book entailed was very enjoyable for Kevin (who is just a big kid at heart). His passion for creativity started at a very young age. As he grew older, his drawing and coloring turned into taking Art classes throughout his high school years, in which he graduated from Southern Wells H.S. in 1990.

Kevin was born in Wells County, Indiana in 1972 and still resides there today. Loved ones in his life are, his wife Tonya, kids Jordan (RIP), Darren, Kirtlyn, and Jazlyn. Oh, and we can't forget the house cat Sage.

Some of Kevin's interests consist of his kids' activities, drawing, watching some football and of course basketball being from the Hoosier State! Other interests are building projects in his shop, enjoying good old cartoons, tv shows, and movies, collecting vintage toys, superheroes, and listening to rock music.

Kevin hopes to continue growing as an illustrator and looks forward to working on many more children's books in the future.

Website–www.kevingillum-illustrations.com

Email–kevingillum.illustrations@gmail.com

Instagram–@kevingillum_illustrations

Twitter–@IllustrationsKG

Facebook–Kevin Gillum Illustrations

Printed in the United States
By Bookmasters